The UNITED STATES PRESIDENTS

Woodrow

WILSON

BreAnn Rumsch

Big Buddy Books
An Imprint of Abdo Publishing
abdopublishing.com

abdopublishing.com

Printed in the United States of America, North Mankato, Minnesota
062016
092016

THIS BOOK CONTAINS
RECYCLED MATERIALS

Design: Sarah DeYoung, Mighty Media, Inc.
Production: Mighty Media, Inc.
Editor: Rebecca Felix
Cover Photograph: Getty Images
Interior Photographs: AP Images (pp. 6, 7, 9, 21, 27, 29); Corbis (pp. 11, 19); Getty Images (p. 17);
    Library of Congress (pp. 5, 13, 15, 23, 25)

Cataloging-in-Publication Data

Names: Rumsch, BreAnn, author.
Title: Woodrow Wilson / by BreAnn Rumsch.
Description: Minneapolis, MN : Abdo Publishing, [2017] | Series: United States
    presidents | Includes bibliographical references and index.
Identifiers: LCCN 2015957562 | ISBN 9781680781236 (lib. bdg.) |
    ISBN 9781680775433 (ebook)
Subjects: LCSH: Wilson, Woodrow, 1856-1924--Juvenile literature. | Presidents-
    -United States--Biography--Juvenile literature. | United States--Politics and
    government--1913-1921--Juvenile literature.
Classification: DDC 973.913/092 [B]--dc23
LC record available at http://lccn.loc.gov/2015957562

Contents

Woodrow Wilson 4

Timeline 6

Young Tommy 8

Off to College 10

Teacher to Leader 14

Honest Governor 18

President Wilson 20

World War I 24

After Politics 28

Office of the President 30

Presidents and Their Terms 34

Glossary .38

Websites .39

Index 40

Woodrow Wilson

Woodrow Wilson was the twenty-eighth president of the United States. Before becoming president, Wilson served as governor of New Jersey. He was elected US president in 1912. President Wilson served two terms.

During his time as president, Wilson created many new laws to help Americans. Wilson led the nation through **World War I**. He also wrote a peace plan that many world leaders **praised** him for. Wilson's honest, fair leadership made him one of America's greatest presidents.

Timeline

1856
On December 28, Thomas Woodrow Wilson was born in Staunton, Virginia.

1913
On March 4, Wilson became the twenty-eighth US president.

1910
Wilson was elected governor of New Jersey.

1916
Wilson was reelected president.

1919

Wilson signed the **Treaty** of Versailles on June 28.

1924

On February 3, Woodrow Wilson died in Washington, DC.

1917

On April 2, Wilson asked Congress to **declare** war on Germany. Four days later, the United States entered **World War I**.

1920

Wilson won the **Nobel Peace Prize** for founding the League of Nations.

7

Young Tommy

Thomas Woodrow Wilson was born in Staunton, Virginia, on December 28, 1856. He was called Tommy. Tommy did not attend school until he was 13 years old. Before then, his father taught him at home.

★ FAST FACTS ★

Born: December 28, 1856

Wives: Ellen Louise Axson (1860–1914), Edith Bolling Galt (1872–1961)

Children: three

Political Party: Democrat

Age at Inauguration: 56

Years Served: 1913–1921

Vice President: Thomas R. Marshall

Died: February 3, 1924, age 67

Thomas Woodrow Wilson's birthplace in Staunton, Virginia

Off to College

In 1873, Wilson entered Davidson College in North Carolina. He studied there for one year. Then, he left school.

Wilson returned to college in 1875. He attended the College of New Jersey in Princeton, New Jersey. The school later changed its name to Princeton University.

Wilson **graduated** from Princeton in 1879. Then he attended the University of Virginia Law School. In 1882, Wilson opened a law office in Georgia.

Wilson was ranked thirty-eighth in his graduating Princeton class of 106 students.

11

The next year, Wilson met Ellen Louise Axson. They soon fell in love. Meanwhile, Wilson realized he did not want to practice law. So, he closed his law office to study to be a college **professor**.

In 1883, Wilson began taking classes at Johns Hopkins University in Maryland. In 1885, Wilson wrote his first book. He and Ellen married that same year.

Wilson **graduated** from Johns Hopkins in 1886. Soon after, he stopped using the name Thomas. From then on, he called himself Woodrow Wilson.

Ellen Louise
Axson Wilson

Teacher to Leader

In 1886, the Wilsons moved to Bryn Mawr, Pennsylvania. There, Wilson took a job teaching history at Bryn Mawr College. The Wilsons had their first daughter, Margaret, that year. Jessie was born in 1887, and Eleanor in 1889.

In 1888, Wilson became a **professor** at Wesleyan University in Connecticut. He published a textbook on government in 1889. The next year, Wilson became a law professor at Princeton.

Mr. and Mrs. Wilson (*center*) with their three daughters. Wilson liked reading aloud to his daughters. He also enjoyed playing games with them.

Wilson quickly became Princeton's most popular teacher. In 1902, the school elected Wilson as its president. A few years later, he created a new way of teaching. It brought teachers and students together in small classes.

Wilson's leadership at Princeton made him famous. Because of this success, some people thought he would make a good **politician**. **Democrat** James Smith Jr. **nominated** Wilson for governor. In 1910, Wilson won the election.

As Princeton's president, Wilson doubled the number of teachers. He also improved the courses the school offered.

Honest Governor

Wilson worked hard as governor. He passed new election laws. Wilson also fought for school **reform**. Wilson was a successful governor. This soon earned him national attention.

In 1912, the **Democrats** chose Wilson to run for president. During his campaign, Wilson promised many things. He wanted to reduce **tariffs** and reorganize the US banking system. Voters liked Wilson's ideas. They elected him president.

While campaigning for president, Wilson traveled around the country.

President Wilson

Wilson took office on March 4, 1913. He wanted to keep his campaign promises. So, he immediately began working with Congress to pass new laws.

Congress passed the Underwood **Tariff** Act. It reduced tariffs. It also made goods cheaper for Americans.

Reducing tariffs meant the government would make less money. So, Congress passed the Sixteenth **Amendment**. It required Americans to pay an **income** tax.

PRESIDENT WILSON'S CABINET

First Term
March 4, 1913–March 4, 1917

- ★ **STATE:** William Jennings Bryan, Robert Lansing (from June 23, 1915)
- ★ **TREASURY:** William G. McAdoo
- ★ **WAR:** Lindley M. Garrison, Newton D. Baker (from March 9, 1916)
- ★ **NAVY:** Josephus Daniels
- ★ **ATTORNEY GENERAL:** James C. McReynolds, Thomas W. Gregory (from September 3, 1914)
- ★ **INTERIOR:** Franklin K. Lane
- ★ **AGRICULTURE:** David F. Houston
- ★ **COMMERCE:** William C. Redfield
- ★ **LABOR:** William B. Wilson

Wilson officially became president at the US Capitol building in Washington, DC.

Second Term
March 4, 1917–March 4, 1921

- ★ **STATE:** Robert Lansing, Bainbridge Colby (from March 23, 1920)
- ★ **TREASURY:** William G. McAdoo, Carter Glass (from December 16, 1918), David F. Houston (from February 2, 1920)
- ★ **WAR:** Newton D. Baker
- ★ **NAVY:** Josephus Daniels
- ★ **ATTORNEY GENERAL:** Thomas W. Gregory, A. Mitchell Palmer (from March 5, 1919)
- ★ **INTERIOR:** Franklin K. Lane, John B. Payne (from March 13, 1920)
- ★ **AGRICULTURE:** David F. Houston, Edwin T. Meredith (from February 2, 1920)
- ★ **COMMERCE:** William C. Redfield, Joshua W. Alexander (from December 16, 1919)
- ★ **LABOR:** William B. Wilson

Meanwhile, a war had begun. **World War I** started in Europe in July 1914. President Wilson promised to keep the United States out of the war.

Soon after the war began, Wilson's wife died. Wilson was sad and lonely. Then, in 1915, Wilson met Edith Bolling Galt. The two married December 15 of that year.

President Wilson ran for reelection in 1916. Voters were glad Wilson had kept America out of World War I. He was reelected.

★ SUPREME COURT ★ APPOINTMENTS

James C. McReynolds: 1914

Louis Brandeis: 1916

John H. Clarke: 1916

Wilson and his second wife,
Edith Bolling Galt Wilson

World War I

During Wilson's second term, Germany began attacking US passenger and merchant ships. Germany's actions angered Americans. On April 2, 1917, Wilson asked Congress to **declare** war on Germany. Four days later, the United States entered **World War I**.

In January 1918, Wilson gave a speech called Fourteen Points. In it, he laid out a peace plan. An important part of the plan was creating the League of Nations. This group was meant to help keep peace worldwide.

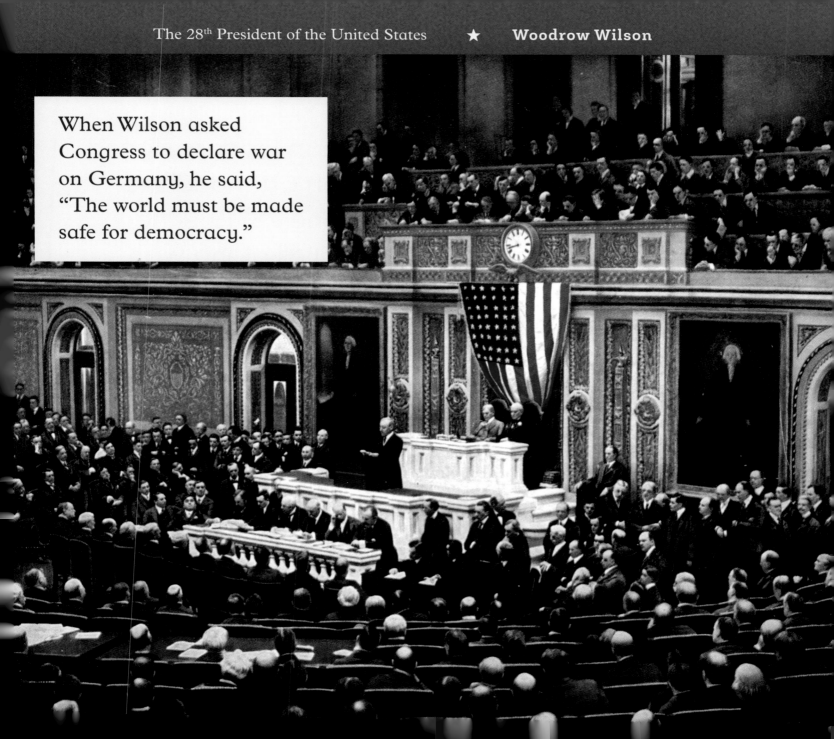

When Wilson asked Congress to declare war on Germany, he said, "The world must be made safe for democracy."

On November 11, 1918, German leaders signed an **armistice**. Soon after, Wilson attended the Paris Peace Conference. On June 28, 1919, he signed the the **Treaty** of Versailles along with other world leaders. The treaty officially ended **World War I**.

Wilson returned to Washington, DC. There, he had a **stroke** that left him **paralyzed**. He did not run in the 1920 election. Later that year, Wilson received the **Nobel Peace Prize** for founding the League of Nations.

★ DID YOU KNOW? ★

President Wilson's image is on the $100,000 bill. However, it is no longer used.

In Paris, Wilson (*far right*) met with (*left to right*) Vittorio Orlando of Italy, David Lloyd George of Great Britain, and Georges Clemenceau of France.

After Politics

In 1921, Wilson left the White House. For the next three years, he led a quiet life in Washington, DC. On February 3, 1924, Woodrow Wilson died in his sleep. He was buried in Washington Cathedral in Washington, DC.

Wilson led America through a troubled time. And he helped end **World War I**. Today, he is best remembered for helping create the League of Nations. It led to the creation of the **United Nations**. In it, Woodrow Wilson's vision for world peace lives on.

The house in Washington, DC, where Wilson lived after his presidency

Office of the President

Branches of Government

The US government has three branches. They are the executive, legislative, and judicial branches. Each branch has some power over the others. This is called a system of checks and balances.

★ **Executive Branch**

The executive branch enforces laws. It is made up of the president, the vice president, and the president's cabinet. The president represents the United States around the world. He or she also signs bills into law and leads the military.

★ **Legislative Branch**

The legislative branch makes laws, maintains the military, and regulates trade. It also has the power to declare war. This branch includes the Senate and the House of Representatives. Together, these two houses form Congress.

★ **Judicial Branch**

The judicial branch interprets laws. It is made up of district courts, courts of appeals, and the Supreme Court. District courts try cases. Sometimes people disagree with a trial's outcome. Then he or she may appeal. If a court of appeals supports the ruling, a person may appeal to the Supreme Court.

Qualifications for Office

To be president, a candidate must be at least 35 years old. The person must be a natural-born US citizen. He or she must also have lived in the United States for at least 14 years.

Electoral College

The US presidential election is an indirect election. Voters from each state choose electors. These electors represent their state in the Electoral College. Each elector has one electoral vote. Electors cast their vote for the candidate with the highest number of votes from people in their state. A candidate must receive the majority of Electoral College votes to win.

Term of Office

Each president may be elected to two four-year terms. The presidential election is held on the Tuesday after the first Monday in November. The president is sworn in on January 20 of the following year. At that time, he or she takes the oath of office.
It states:

> I do solemnly swear (or affirm) that I will faithfully execute the office of President of the United States, and will to the best of my ability, preserve, protect and defend the Constitution of the United States.

Line of Succession

The Presidential Succession Act of 1947 states who becomes president if the president cannot serve. The vice president is first in the line. Next are the Speaker of the House and the President Pro Tempore of the Senate. It may happen that none of these individuals is able to serve. Then the office falls to the president's cabinet members. They would take office in the order in which each department was created:

Secretary of State

Secretary of the Treasury

Secretary of Defense

Attorney General

Secretary of the Interior

Secretary of Agriculture

Secretary of Commerce

Secretary of Labor

Secretary of Health and Human Services

Secretary of Housing and Urban Development

Secretary of Transportation

Secretary of Energy

Secretary of Education

Secretary of Veterans Affairs

Secretary of Homeland Security

Benefits

★ While in office, the president receives a salary. It is $400,000 per year. He or she lives in the White House. The president also has 24-hour Secret Service protection.

★ The president may travel on a Boeing 747 jet. This special jet is called Air Force One. It can hold 70 passengers. It has kitchens, a dining room, sleeping areas, and more. Air Force One can fly halfway around the world before needing to refuel. It can even refuel in flight!

★ When the president travels by car, he or she uses Cadillac One. It is a Cadillac Deville that has been modified. The car has heavy armor and communications systems. The president may even take Cadillac One along when visiting other countries.

★ The president also travels on a helicopter. It is called Marine One. It may also be taken along when the president visits other countries.

★ Sometimes the president needs to get away with family and friends. Camp David is the official presidential retreat. It is located in Maryland. The US Navy maintains the retreat. The US Marine Corps keeps it secure. The camp offers swimming, tennis, golf, and hiking.

★ When the president leaves office, he or she receives lifetime Secret Service protection. He or she also receives a yearly pension of $203,700. The former president also receives money for office space, supplies, and staff.

33

PRESIDENTS AND THEIR TERMS

PRESIDENT	PARTY	TOOK OFFICE	LEFT OFFICE	TERMS SERVED	VICE PRESIDENT
George Washington	None	April 30, 1789	March 4, 1797	Two	John Adams
John Adams	Federalist	March 4, 1797	March 4, 1801	One	Thomas Jefferson
Thomas Jefferson	Democratic-Republican	March 4, 1801	March 4, 1809	Two	Aaron Burr, George Clinton
James Madison	Democratic-Republican	March 4, 1809	March 4, 1817	Two	George Clinton, Elbridge Gerry
James Monroe	Democratic-Republican	March 4, 1817	March 4, 1825	Two	Daniel D. Tompkins
John Quincy Adams	Democratic-Republican	March 4, 1825	March 4, 1829	One	John C. Calhoun
Andrew Jackson	Democrat	March 4, 1829	March 4, 1837	Two	John C. Calhoun, Martin Van Buren
Martin Van Buren	Democrat	March 4, 1837	March 4, 1841	One	Richard M. Johnson
William H. Harrison	Whig	March 4, 1841	April 4, 1841	Died During First Term	John Tyler
John Tyler	Whig	April 6, 1841	March 4, 1845	Completed Harrison's Term	Office Vacant
James K. Polk	Democrat	March 4, 1845	March 4, 1849	One	George M. Dallas
Zachary Taylor	Whig	March 5, 1849	July 9, 1850	Died During First Term	Millard Fillmore

PRESIDENT	PARTY	TOOK OFFICE	LEFT OFFICE	TERMS SERVED	VICE PRESIDENT
Millard Fillmore	Whig	July 10, 1850	March 4, 1853	Completed Taylor's Term	Office Vacant
Franklin Pierce	Democrat	March 4, 1853	March 4, 1857	One	William R.D. King
James Buchanan	Democrat	March 4, 1857	March 4, 1861	One	John C. Breckinridge
Abraham Lincoln	Republican	March 4, 1861	April 15, 1865	Served One Term, Died During Second Term	Hannibal Hamlin, Andrew Johnson
Andrew Johnson	Democrat	April 15, 1865	March 4, 1869	Completed Lincoln's Second Term	Office Vacant
Ulysses S. Grant	Republican	March 4, 1869	March 4, 1877	Two	Schuyler Colfax, Henry Wilson
Rutherford B. Hayes	Republican	March 3, 1877	March 4, 1881	One	William A. Wheeler
James A. Garfield	Republican	March 4, 1881	September 19, 1881	Died During First Term	Chester Arthur
Chester Arthur	Republican	September 20, 1881	March 4, 1885	Completed Garfield's Term	Office Vacant
Grover Cleveland	Democrat	March 4, 1885	March 4, 1889	One	Thomas A. Hendricks
Benjamin Harrison	Republican	March 4, 1889	March 4, 1893	One	Levi P. Morton
Grover Cleveland	Democrat	March 4, 1893	March 4, 1897	One	Adlai E. Stevenson
William McKinley	Republican	March 4, 1897	September 14, 1901	Served One Term, Died During Second Term	Garret A. Hobart, Theodore Roosevelt

PRESIDENT	PARTY	TOOK OFFICE	LEFT OFFICE	TERMS SERVED	VICE PRESIDENT
Theodore Roosevelt	Republican	September 14, 1901	March 4, 1909	Completed McKinley's Second Term, Served One Term	Office Vacant, Charles Fairbanks
William Taft	Republican	March 4, 1909	March 4, 1913	One	James S. Sherman
Woodrow Wilson	Democrat	March 4, 1913	March 4, 1921	Two	Thomas R. Marshall
Warren G. Harding	Republican	March 4, 1921	August 2, 1923	Died During First Term	Calvin Coolidge
Calvin Coolidge	Republican	August 3, 1923	March 4, 1929	Completed Harding's Term, Served One Term	Office Vacant, Charles Dawes
Herbert Hoover	Republican	March 4, 1929	March 4, 1933	One	Charles Curtis
Franklin D. Roosevelt	Democrat	March 4, 1933	April 12, 1945	Served Three Terms, Died During Fourth Term	John Nance Garner, Henry A. Wallace, Harry S. Truman
Harry S. Truman	Democrat	April 12, 1945	January 20, 1953	Completed Roosevelt's Fourth Term, Served One Term	Office Vacant, Alben Barkley
Dwight D. Eisenhower	Republican	January 20, 1953	January 20, 1961	Two	Richard Nixon
John F. Kennedy	Democrat	January 20, 1961	November 22, 1963	Died During First Term	Lyndon B. Johnson
Lyndon B. Johnson	Democrat	November 22, 1963	January 20, 1969	Completed Kennedy's Term, Served One Term	Office Vacant, Hubert H. Humphrey
Richard Nixon	Republican	January 20, 1969	August 9, 1974	Completed First Term, Resigned During Second Term	Spiro T. Agnew, Gerald Ford

PRESIDENT	PARTY	TOOK OFFICE	LEFT OFFICE	TERMS SERVED	VICE PRESIDENT
Gerald Ford	Republican	August 9, 1974	January 20, 1977	Completed Nixon's Second Term	Nelson A. Rockefeller
Jimmy Carter	Democrat	January 20, 1977	January 20, 1981	One	Walter Mondale
Ronald Reagan	Republican	January 20, 1981	January 20, 1989	Two	George H.W. Bush
George H.W. Bush	Republican	January 20, 1989	January 20, 1993	One	Dan Quayle
Bill Clinton	Democrat	January 20, 1993	January 20, 2001	Two	Al Gore
George W. Bush	Republican	January 20, 2001	January 20, 2009	Two	Dick Cheney
Barack Obama	Democrat	January 20, 2009	January 20, 2017	Two	Joe Biden

"The business of government is to organize the common interest against the special interests." Woodrow Wilson

★ WRITE TO THE PRESIDENT ★

You may write to the president at:
The White House
1600 Pennsylvania Avenue NW
Washington, DC 20500

You may e-mail the president at:
comments@whitehouse.gov

37

Glossary

amendment—a change to a country's or a state's constitution.

armistice—an agreement to stop fighting a war.

declare—to officially announce something.

Democrat—a member of the Democratic political party.

graduate (GRA-juh-wayt)—to complete a level of schooling.

income—money that is earned, such as a wage or salary.

Nobel Peace Prize—an award given for doing something to help make peace in the world.

nominate—to name as a possible winner.

paralyzed (PEHR-uh-lized)—affected with a loss of feeling or motion in part of the body.

politics—the art or science of government. Something referring to politics is political. A person who is active in politics is a politician.

praise—to give approval or admiration.

professor—a teacher at a college or university.

reform—to remove problems and make something better.

stroke—a medical problem caused by lack of blood flow to the brain. Strokes are serious. They may cause brain damage or death.

tariff—the taxes a government puts on imported or exported goods.

treaty—an agreement made between two or more groups.

United Nations—a group of nations formed in 1945. Its goals are peace, human rights, security, and social and economic development.

World War I—a war fought in Europe from 1914 to 1918.

★ **WEBSITES** ★

To learn more about the US Presidents, visit **booklinks.abdopublishing.com**. These links are routinely monitored and updated to provide the most current information available.

Index

birth   **6, 8, 9**

Bryn Mawr College   **14**

childhood   **8, 9**

Congress, US   **7, 20, 24, 25**

death   **7, 8, 28**

Democratic Party   **8, 16, 18**

education   **8, 10, 11, 12**

family   **8, 12, 13 14, 15, 22, 23**

Fourteen Points   **24**

Georgia   **10**

Germany   **7, 24, 25, 26**

governor   **4, 6, 16, 18**

health   **26**

inauguration   **6, 8, 20**

Johns Hopkins University   **12**

League of Nations   **7, 24, 26, 28**

Nobel Peace Prize   **7, 26**

Paris Peace Conference   **26, 27**

Princeton University   **10, 11, 14, 16, 17**

Sixteenth Amendment   **20**

Smith, James, Jr.   **16**

Underwood Tariff Act   **20**

United Nations   **28**

University of Virginia   **10**

Versailles, Treaty of   **7, 26, 27**

Wesleyan University   **14**

World War I   **4, 7, 22, 24, 25, 26, 27, 28**